Asian
LEICESTER

Asian
LEICESTER

John Martin & Gurharpal Singh

with support from *David Clark*

SUTTON PUBLISHING

Sutton Publishing Limited
Phoenix Mill · Thrupp · Stroud
Gloucestershire · GL5 2BU

First published 2002

Frontispiece: Hartington Road, 1989.
(*Leicester Mercury*)

British Library Cataloguing in Publication Data
A catalogue record for this book is available from the
British Library.

ISBN 0-7509-2226-5

Typeset in 10.5/13.5 Photina.
Typesetting and origination by
Sutton Publishing Limited.
Printed and bound in England by
J.H. Haynes & Co. Ltd, Sparkford.

We could not hope in the space of a single book to produce a comprehensive survey of Asian Leicester and will inevitably have omitted individuals, organizations and places that are an integral part of the city. This book is not intended as a general guide or as a gazetteer but as a limited first effort.

The people whose photographs appear in this book do not constitute an exhaustive list of those who have contributed to the development of the local community. Instead they are incidental to the story recounted here, which is intended to demonstrate the positive and valuable contribution the Asian community has played in the development of the city.

We hope readers will share the authors' pleasure in studying a rich and diverse city and the people who have helped to shape it. The surviving and available pictorial evidence offers an immediate, if partial, view of the development of Leicester and is designed to enhance our understanding of the different cultures.

Sikh procession past
Leicester's clock tower,
c. 1990. (*Leicester Mercury*)

CONTENTS

A model elephant operated by two men leads a Diwali procession through the streets of Leicester, 1989. (*Leicester Mercury*)

INTRODUCTION

In popular imagination Leicester is most commonly associated with its Asian community. The city which was once described by a local historian 'as wholly uninteresting' and by J.B. Priestley as 'lacking in character', is today internationally recognized as a model of civic multiculturalism, and calls itself a 'place of many surprises'. Over several decades a parochial East Midlands market town was transformed into a modern multicultural city which has received accolades from the United Nations. The process began with the arrival of New Commonwealth migrants after the Second World War and involved decades of challenge and adaptation. As the city enters the twenty-first century, the Asian community has become much more self-confident, increasingly conscious of its role in local, national and international affairs.*

This book records in photographs the contribution of Asians to the development of Leicester since 1945. It looks at Asian settlement, work, education, religion, community institutions, the family, leisure, culture and public life. As far as we are aware, there has been no previous systematic research on the social history of the Asian community in Leicester. Specialists have examined single-issue areas – housing, racism, ethnic businesses, local politics – but an overall sense of community development has been missing from their accounts. *Asian Leicester* seeks to fill this important gap by outlining future areas of research into a relatively neglected area of twentieth-century British urban history. (For one of the more informed studies already available on the city see D. Nash and D. Reeder, *Leicester in the Twentieth Century* (Stroud, Sutton Publishing, 1993.)

Today's Leicester is one of the most ethnically diverse cities in the European Union. Out of a population of 283,000 included in the results of the 1991 census, over 28.5 per cent are classified as of 'ethnicity originating outside the United Kingdom'. Of these 22 per cent (60,600) are from India, 1 per cent (3,000) from Pakistan, 0.8 per cent (2,000) from Bangladesh, and 2.8 per cent (6,600) are of African/Caribbean origin. This figure excludes 3,000 Chinese, 3,000 Poles, 2,000 Ukrainians, 3,000 Serbians, 500 Lithuanians, 250 Vietnamese, 500 Jews and other minorities, as well as more than 5,000 overseas students resident in the city during the academic year. The rate of settlement and growth has not tailed off. It is reasonable to assume that given the age distribution of the Asian population, the arrival of new migrants (East Africa),

---

* By 'Asian' we mean all those of South Asian ethnic origin, even if they were part of the South Asian diaspora before settling in Leicester.

and internal migration within Great Britain, the size of Leicester's Asian population will continue to increase. Some estimates suggest that in the next few years the Asian and Afro-Caribbean population will represent about 40–50 per cent of the total population.

In the aftermath of the Second World War there was little indication that Leicester was on the threshold of a major cultural change. In 1951 the Asian population of the city was only 624. It would seem that most of these people settled in Leicester after 1945 because there is little recorded evidence of earlier presence. Indeed, before the war contacts between Leicester and people from areas that subsequently became the New Commonwealth were limited to tours by the local regiments (Leicester Tigers), visiting political leaders, students and the occasional early migrant. Of the political leaders, it is said Mahatma Gandhi intended to visit the city during the Roundtable Talks of 1932 but was unable to keep his appointment. Former soldiers in the Indian Army and itinerant visitors made up the main bulk of Leicester's Asian population before 1945. The Indian Workers' Association (IWA) was founded in nearby Coventry in 1938, and it soon became the main point of contact for settlers from the Indian subcontinent who were keen to establish links and remain in touch with developments in India.

The first settlers who were to play a key part in future migration arrived after the Second World War. Two key events triggered this movement. First, the independence of India was followed by the partition of the province of Punjab between India and Pakistan. This dislocated over 10 million people. Punjab had had a history of outward migration since the nineteenth century; and given their central role in the Indian Army, many former soldiers who had seen service overseas decided to start new lives in foreign countries. The other key factor was the establishment of the right to settle in Great Britain. The Nationality Act (1948) technically gave every Commonwealth citizen the right to move to the 'mother country'. Given the postwar demand for workers, changes in Commonwealth countries, and the dislocation brought about by the Second World War, there were significant incentives to migrate. Nevertheless, many barriers had to be overcome before migrants could arrive in Britain. The early settlers played a crucial role in transmitting information about work, immigration rules, and settlement difficulties.

Migration to the city was hastened by the Commonwealth and Immigration Act (1962), which restricted the right of Commonwealth citizens to settle in Britain. After 1962 migrants needed a work voucher in order to ensure entry to the country. Fears of more restrictive immigration legislation led to pre-emptive migration and family reunions.

By 1961 the New Commonwealth population in the city had increased to 4,624. Most of these migrants settled in Highfields and the Belgrave area where rented accommodation was plentiful. The St Peter's Estate in Highfields was favoured by Afro-Caribbeans, while Indians and Pakistanis chose properties near the Spinney Hill Park and Belgrave Road where affordable private housing was available. Enterprising migrants were able to purchase properties that were often used for multiple-occupancy.

Gallowtree Gate, the central shopping area of Leicester, 1958. (*Leicester Mercury*)

By the early 1960s the Asian settlers had established a semblance of community life. A Sikh gurdwara was founded on New Walk and soon became the centre of community life. (It was the forerunner of the present gurdwara on Holy Bones.) The IWA became more active in organizing migrants to campaign on issues of racism, culture and work. In 1965 a bhangra club was formed which rented rooms on Regents Road. At the heart of the community in Highfields, two inner-city cinemas, the Melbourne and the Evington, began to show Indian films on Sundays. Visits to religious places on Sunday mornings were often followed by the midday or afternoon viewing of the latest Bollywood blockbuster.

Within Highfields the Imperial public house and its immediate vicinity became the place for shopping, socializing and meeting new arrivals. The Imperial served as an unofficial community centre. Spinney Hill Park, near Imperial and Victoria Park, became the base for many sports clubs – hockey was a particular favourite. In 1966 the Indian Sports Association (ISA) was formed which annually sponsored a sports festival held at the Saffron Lane Stadium. This became a major event and teams from all over Europe participated. In 1968 the ISA hosted a visit by the Indian national hockey team which had competed in the Mexico Olympics.

The Asian population of the city increased dramatically during the 1960s. In addition to family reunions, the late '60s saw the beginnings of East African Asian migration. This movement was prompted by Africanization – the achievement of

Eid gathering in Victoria Park, 1990. (*Leicester Mercury*)

independence by African countries and the resulting pressure on the population of Asian descent to choose between British and local citizenship. The exodus from Kenya resulted in many Kenyan Asians finding their way to Leicester. In 1971, before the arrival of migrants from Uganda, Leicester's Asian population was 20,190.

In 1972 General Idi Amin decided to expel the Asian population of Uganda. Because many East Africans had already moved to Leicester, the City Council anticipated more arrivals and took out adverts in the Ugandan press discouraging refugees with a right to settle in Great Britain from making Leicester their destination. Some commentators believed that these warnings had the opposite effect because they attracted attention to Leicester. Whatever the case, the arrival of Ugandan Asians marked a fundamental change in the character of the city.

By 1981 the New Commonwealth population of Leicester had seen an almost three-fold increase to 59,709. This rapid growth created serious political, economic and administrative challenges – challenges that ultimately affected the nature of all civic institutions in the city.

Initially the arrival of Ugandan Asians set off a wave of racism. Hostility to coloured immigrants had been a constant feature of Asian settlement but the early 1970s saw the local growth of the National Front which established a base among the white working class of the city. In the February 1974 general elections the National Front secured 7.4 per cent of the vote in the constituency of Leicester East, 6.4 per cent in Leicester West, and 3 per cent in Leicester South. The Front did better in local elections. In 1976 it came within 61 votes of victory in the Abbey Ward and gained 18 per cent of the total vote in the city. The Front's influence was at its peak in the mid-1970s but declined after the general elections of 1979.

The atmosphere of racial hostility created by the National Front's activities manifested itself in other ways. The Imperial Typewriters strike in 1974 became a symbol of the deeply entrenched racism within the city and its labour movement which was seen as unresponsive to the needs of black workers. This bitter strike, which attracted national attention, was followed by the Mansfield Hosiery dispute. The activities of the National Front in the city were challenged by the local chapters of the IWA, the Anti-Nazi League and the Inter-Racial Solidarity Campaign (an alliance of activists within the labour movement and civic life).

Anti-racist mobilization in the mid-1970s had a strong influence on the local Labour Party. Young activists like Peter Soulsby recognized the importance of the issue which was reflected in major national developments, for example, the Race Relations Act (1976). The new law placed the onus on local authorities to improve race relations. It also created the Commission for Racial Equality to police the legislation. But the displacement of 'Old Labour' was gradual and took almost a decade. It was not until the early 1980s that the 'new left' with its commitment to a multiracial city was firmly in power. By 1983 there were nine Labour Asian councillors on the City Council, representing inner-city wards in Highfields and Belgrave. After this political success the Labour Party undertook an audit of the council's services. The findings were used to target services more effectively, to increase the number of non-whites on the City Council's workforce to reflect the

Members of the Indian Workers Association in London, 1990s. (*Sital Gill*)

proportion of non-whites in the population, and to reformulate general policies in areas such as cultural policy.

Against the backdrop of inner-city riots of 1981, evidence of high levels of unemployment among Asian and Afro-Caribbean youth was used to attract inner-city grants from central government. This funding, and the patronage associated with its distribution, became focus of the politics of the new Asian councillors.

In the 1980s, with the solid support of the Asian community, Leicester became a Labour Party stronghold. In 1987 all three parliamentary seats were won by the Labour Party. Keith Vaz captured Leicester East to become the first Asian MP since 1923.

During these years Leicester became a city of Asian festivals. The biggest of these is Diwali (the Hindu festival of light), which is celebrated every October in Belgrave's 'Golden Mile'. This is the largest celebration of Diwali outside India, and often attracts crowds of up to 60,000. Other religious occasions, Eid and Vaisakhi, are also celebrated in areas of majority Muslim and Sikh settlement in Highfields and Evington Road.

In addition to supporting religious and cultural festivals, the City Council has helped Asian civic associations. There are over 400 ethnic minority associations. Many have regular contacts with the City Council and carry out particular services for the local authority and central government. Some work in housing, age concern, women's projects, youth or retraining. Many voluntary groups have been successful in generating their own resources and function as sub-agents for the council in administering projects. The voluntary sector has become a powerful lobby which stands outside institutionalized politics.

The 1990s witnessed a gradual change in the relationship between the Labour Party and the Asian community in Leicester. As the power of local government declined, communities and associations have been compelled to rely on their own resources to sustain their activities. At the same time within the City Council the language of multiculturalism has increasingly given way to 'corporate equality' and the 'management of diversity'. Although the Labour Party continues to command most of the Asian vote in the city, there is some disaffection among certain sections. In some ways this perhaps reflects the ideological exhaustion of anti-racism and the inability of the local authority to meet the new challenge of local diversity. It may also signal the emergence of political preferences beyond the traditional loyalty to the Labour Party.

While the local Labour Party played an important role in changing the political climate in the city from the 1970s onwards, it is the work and efforts of local Asians that are the root of Leicester's success. This is evident in the emergence of a very competitive Asian business sector in retailing, hosiery and garment manufacturing. There are over 10,000 registered Asian businesses. Many of these were formed in response to the manufacturing slump of the 1980s as a means of self-employment. Since then they have grown to displace the typical image of an Asian corner shop. Contemporary Leicester boasts some of the most successful Asian businesses in Great Britain and many of them have overseas trading links, particularly with Europe, South Asia and North America. The Belgrave Road has emerged as a shopping and

An aerial view of Highfields with the Central Mosque in the foreground. (*Vasant Kalyani*)

commercial centre of international renown. Its vast array of stores has made it a popular attraction for Asians from all over Britain who often prefer to shop in Leicester for special occasions like weddings rather than make the costly journey to South Asia.

The growing self-confidence of Asians in Leicester and their attachment to the city is noticeable in the changing patterns of settlement. The traditional areas – Belgrave, Highfields – remain popular but some Asians have moved to the leafy suburbs of Oadby, Evington and the large residential houses around London Road. Rushey Mead has acted as an overspill area for Belgrave Road. There are also some signs of gradual movement towards the countryside with villages like Great Glen and Birstall becoming popular.

The city has seen a proliferation of places of religious worship. There are several Sikh gurdwaras, Hindu mandirs and Muslim mosques. Prominent among these are the Westbourne Street mandir, Sikh gurdwaras on Holy Bones and Evington Road, the Conduit Street mosque, the Swaminarayan temple on Narborough Road, and the Jain temple on Oxford Street. Religious leaders from India make regular visits to congregations in Leicester. Many sects and orders have a popular following among the city's population.

The city is also the centre of Asian cultural life in Britain. It boasts a thriving cultural community with regular performances at the city's two theatres. There are several dance groups of international renown and these international connections are constantly reinforced because the city has become a permanent venue for actors, singers, writers and artists from India, Pakistan and Bangladesh.

The success of Leicester's Asians continues to attract more settlers. In recent years there have been new arrivals from South Africa, Malawi and Tanzania. Leicester's growing reputation as a city of Asian business has also fuelled much migration within Britain, especially from cities in northern England. Internal migration, however, has not been countered by outward migration by residents of Asian descent. While many professionals have sought job opportunities outside the city, in Europe and North America, others still retain family associations with Leicester. In general, among Asians who grew up in Leicester there is a strong attachment to the city and many return, even after years of living elsewhere.

The genial temper of Leicester makes it an attractive city to live in as well as an ideal location for the most multicultural urban centre in Great Britain. Over the last fifty years the Asian community in Leicester has developed self-confidence and it can face the twenty-first century with a great optimism. Asian Leicester is likely to remain an outstanding example of diversity and ethnic plurality.

1

Settling

An Asian couple with their children outside their house in Highfields, 1960s. (*Manjit Singh Rano*)

Historically India was the brightest jewel in the Crown of Empire that enabled Britain to project itself as a world super-power. India mattered on every occasion – state, official, ceremonial or commemorative. The British revelled in and acclaimed the pomp of the India's princes, praised the courage of her soldiers and boasted of the loyalty of the common masses to the Raj. The origins of opposition to India are recent and are connected with surfacing racist strains in British society.

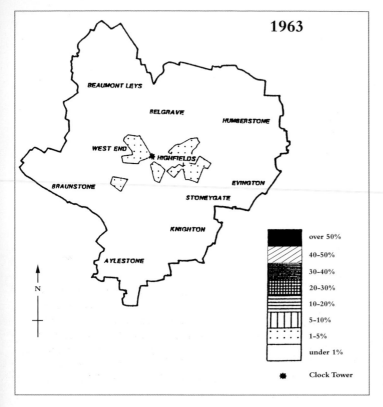

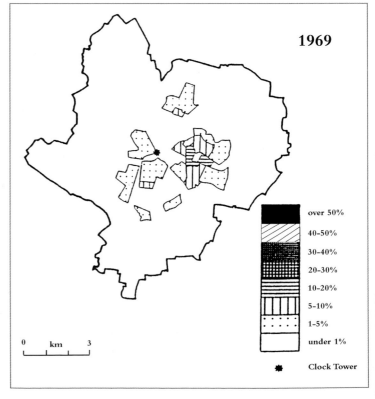

Asian settlement patterns in 1963 (left) and 1969 (below), illustrating the way Asians were geographically concentrated in the city in the 1960s. This concentration reflected the location of relatively low-priced housing and its close proximity to the railway and bus stations. (*Office of Population Censuses and Surveys*)

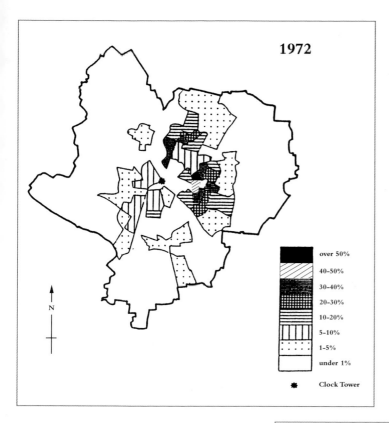

1972

N

over 50%
40–50%
30–40%
20–30%
10–20%
5–10%
1–5%
under 1%

✴ Clock Tower

Following the influx from Uganda, the number of Asians in the city increased rapidly. They were heavily concentrated in the Belgrave and Highfields areas of the city. The top map shows settlement in 1972 and the one below indicates the picture in 1978. (*Office of Population Censuses and Surveys*)

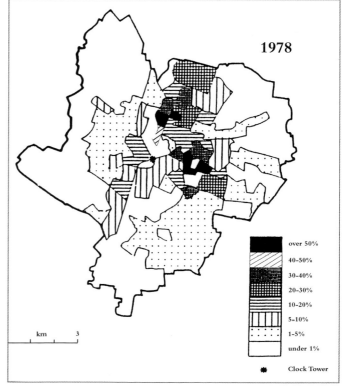

1978

over 50%
40–50%
30–40%
20–30%
10–20%
5–10%
1–5%
under 1%

✴ Clock Tower

km   3

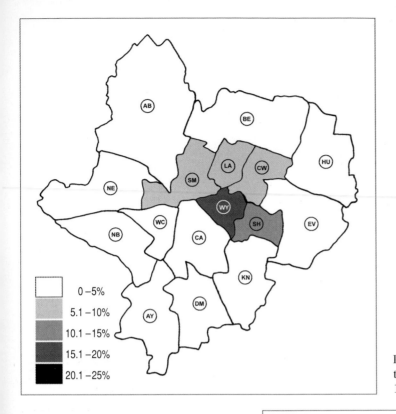

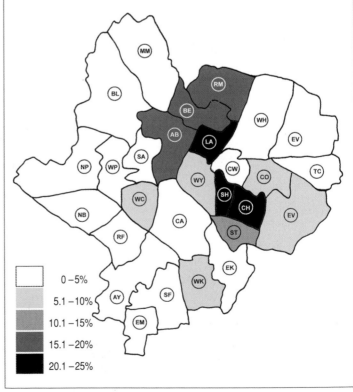

Distribution of those born in India throughout Leicester in 1971 (left) and 1991 (below) by council ward.

KEY

AB	The Abbey
AY	Aylestone
BE	Belgrave
CA	The Castle
CH	Crown Hills
CO	Coleman
CW	Charnwood
DM	De Montfort
EK	East Knighton
EM	Eyres Mansell
EV	Evington
HU	Humberstone
KN	Knighton
LA	Latimer
NE	Newton
NB	N. Braunstone
NP	New Parks
RF	Rowley Fields
SA	St Augustines
SF	Saffron
SH	Spinney Hill
SM	St Margaret's
TC	Thorncourt
WC	Westcotes
WH	West Humberstone
WP	Western Park
WY	Wycliffe

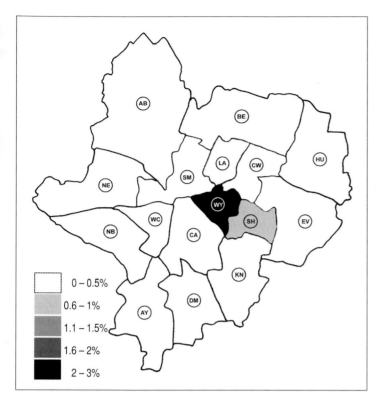

Distribution of those born in Pakistan throughout Leicester in 1971 (left) and 1991 (below) by council ward.

0 – 0.5%
0.6 – 1%
1.1 – 1.5%
1.6 – 2%
2 – 3%

KEY

AB	The Abbey
AY	Aylestone
BE	Belgrave
CA	The Castle
CH	Crown Hills
CO	Coleman
CW	Charnwood
DM	De Montfort
EK	East Knighton
EM	Eyres Mansell
EV	Evington
HU	Humberstone
KN	Knighton
LA	Latimer
NE	Newton
NB	N. Braunstone
NP	New Parks
RF	Rowley Fields
SA	St Augustines
SF	Saffron
SH	Spinney Hill
SM	St Margaret's
TC	Thorncourt
WC	Westcotes
WH	West Humberstone
WP	Western Park
WY	Wycliffe

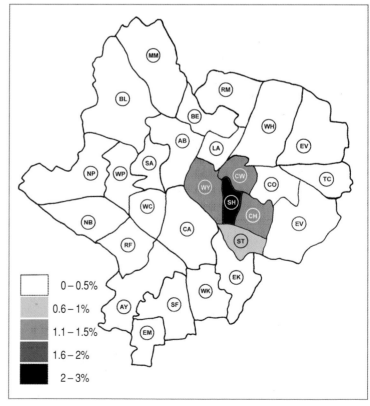

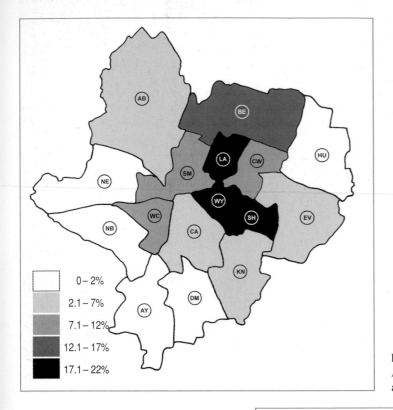

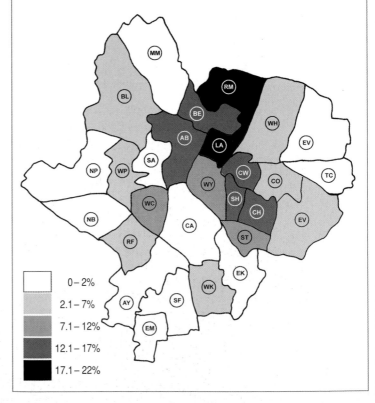

Distribution of those born in Eastern
Africa throughout Leicester in 1981 (left)
and 1991 (below) by council ward.

KEY

AB	The Abbey
AY	Aylestone
BE	Belgrave
CA	The Castle
CO	Coleman
CH	Crown Hills
CW	Charnwood
DM	De Montfort
EK	East Knighton
EM	Eyres Mansell
EV	Evington
HU	Humberstone
KN	Knighton
LA	Latimer
NE	Newton
NB	N. Braunstone
NP	New Parks
RF	Rowley Fields
SA	St Augustines
SF	Saffron
SH	Spinney Hill
SM	St Margaret's
TC	Thorncourt
WC	Westcotes
WH	West Humberstone
WP	Western Park
WY	Wycliffe

Belgrave Gate, looking towards the station and Abbey Park Road from St Mark's Church, April 1953. The area has now been redeveloped by the Asian business community. (*Leicester Record Office*)

Belgrave Road, 1959. This type of property prevailed in the area in the postwar period. (*Leicester Record Office*)

View from the top of London Road, 1961. The railway station is in the distance and the Highfields area is to the right. (*Leicester Record Office*)

Leicester station, 1961. This would have been the point of arrival for most Asians travelling to Leicester in the 1960s. (*Leicester Record Office*)

Typical terraced houses, Highfields, 1962. It was in this area that many Asian people initially settled. (*Manjit Singh Rano*)

A group of Asian children in the mid-1960s. The terraced houses are typical of large areas of central Leicester at the time. (*Manjit Singh Rano*)

An Asian family in a Leicester street, 1963. Most of these properties consisted of two rooms and a back kitchen on the ground floor; stairs set at right angles to the front of the house gave access to three bedrooms. This type of house had often been neglected during the 1950s after the previous inhabitants moved to newly constructed housing estates. (*Manjit Singh Rano*)

AN IMPORTANT ANNOUNCEMENT ON BEHALF OF THE COUNCIL OF THE CITY OF LEICESTER, ENGLAND

The City Council of Leicester, England, believe
that many families in Uganda are
considering moving to Leicester.
if YOU are thinking of doing so it is very
important you should know that
PRESENT CONDITIONS IN THE CITY ARE
VERY DIFFERENT FROM THOSE MET BY
EARLIER SETTLERS. They are:—

HOUSING — several thousands of families are already on
the Council's waiting list.

EDUCATION — hundreds of children are awaiting places in
schools

SOCIAL AND HEALTH SERVICES — already stretched to
the limit

IN YOUR OWN INTERESTS AND THOSE OF YOUR FAMILY YOU SHOULD ACCEPT THE ADVICE OF THE UGANDA RESETTLEMENT BOARD AND NOT COME TO LEICESTER

The local authorities in Birmingham, Bradford, Ealing and Brent responded to the projected arrival of Ugandan Asians with apathy rather than opposition. Leicester City Council decided to advertise in the *Ugandan Argus* on 17 September 1972 urging the population to accept the advice of the Ugandan Settlement Board and not come to Leicester where, it claimed, housing, education and social services were stretched to the limit. (*Val Marett*)

Leicester Mercury

EXTRA

Incorporating the Leicester Evening Mail

Established 1874   THURSDAY, AUGUST 31, 1972   3p

WHITEHALL TOLD: NO MORE —LEICESTER IS FULL UP

Leicester City Council's deputation to the Home Office pictured at London Road station ticket barrier this morning. The Lord Mayor, Alderman Stanley Tomlinson, is handing his ticket to collector Mr. Herbert Northwood, and behind him, are left to right: Alderman Edward Marston (Labour group leader), Mr. R. R. Thornton (Town Clerk), Alderman Kenneth Bowder (Conservative group leader), and Councillor Mrs. Janet Setchfield (assistant Labour group whip).

AS THEY LEFT the Home Office today after talks on Leicester's attitude to an influx of Ugandan Asians, the Corporation's deputation declared: "We told the Minister that Leicester is full up."

Leader of the City Council, Alderman Edward Marston, told a Leicester Mercury Civics Correspondent: "We urged that the Minister should use his influence to direct these people to other towns and cities where they would have more opportunities than in Leicester."

The deputation had spent nearly two hours emphasising Leicester's position — particularly the fact that services like housing, education, health and social services were already fully stretched — to Mr. David Lean, a deputy to the Home Secretary Mr. Robert Carr, who is on holiday in a remote part of Corfu.

Alderman Marston added: "Mr. Lane assured us that due consideration would be given by the Government to our real problems.

"We were able to press on him that Leicester, as far as housing and services are concerned, is full up. And our schools and homes are overcrowded."

DISASTER

Alderman Marston said that it had been pointed out to the deputation that the Asians could not be directed to particular places, but the Minister would do all possible to advise those intending to make for Leicester aware of the great difficulties they would face.

Asked if Mr. Lane had given any promises of money or aid in housing, Alderman Marston commented: "He said this may be available."

Alderman Marston added: "Mr. Lane is going to pass on to Robert Carr all the information we have been able to give him."

Another member of the deputation, Alderman Kenneth Bowder, chairman of the Co-

400 years and now . . . girls

A 400-YEAR-OLD tradition went by the board at Ashby-de-la-Zouch Boys' Grammar School today.

The school, with the motto, "I Byde My Time" and a bull's head as its emblem has admitted girls.

And the Girls' Grammar School of less antiquity and only a few hundred yards away, has admitted boys.

The establishment of coeducational procedures at the two schools has resulted from the amalgamation.

Both buildings are used for mixed classes.

The headmaster of Ashby Boys' Grammar School, Dr. Ronald Allison, said today that during the holidays there had been building at both schools to provide the necessary cloakroom facilities.

"We shall require a little time to settle down under the new system, and like other schools in the county, we are still waiting for extra classrooms and temporary buildings including language laboratories."

operative group, said: "We told the Minister that while as a city we were prepared to help in this great humanitarian disaster, we had already done all we could in absorbing immigrants and that other cities in the country should now make their contribution."

"The immigrants we already have we have learned to accept, and they are making a real contribution to our society but there is little room for any more."

Asked if he were satisfied with the way the talks had gone Alderman Bowder declared: "We are as satisfied as we can be at this time."

Other members of the deputation were the Lord Mayor, Alderman Stanley Tomlinson, the assistant Labour Whip, Councillor Mrs. Jane Setchfield, and the Town Clerk, Mr. R. R. Thornton.

WORRIED

The deputation will report in detail on their visit to the Home Office at tonight's emergency meeting of the City Council, called to discuss what some members have described as "the city's greatest ever crisis".

After the meeting it was learned that a member of the Uganda Resettlement Board will visit Leicester shortly. No date has been set for the visit.

A Ugandan Asian family who have arrived in Leicester penniless appealed today for action from the British Government to safeguard their Ugandan bank accounts and other property left behind.

Mr. Harshi Vadher (22) arrived in Leicester yesterday with his

✱ Continued on Page 19

Mr. Dhanu Vadher, and three-year old Bindu in Leicester today.

Prison officer at Gartree bitten by gang man

GARTREE PRISON, Market Harborough, was back to normal today after a prison officer was bitten in a struggle with a prisoner.

The officer was bitten when a well-known member of one of the big London gangs refused to pay a fine and return to work for his part in the strike.

He was being taken to the punishment block before adjudication was made when there was a struggle and the officer was bitten in his thigh. The prisoner is likely to face further charges.

Prison governor Mr. R. E. Adams said today the rest of the prison inmates were "hard at work."

Some of the officers were upset by the small fines imposed on the strikers but many see the fact that the prisoners had to climb down publicly as a triumph for law and order.

The most significant thing, say the officers, is that the one man's battle has not gained any support and little sympathy from the other 370 inmates.

'Barons' fear

Magistrates were due at the prison today to deal with a man who was involved in an incident in the hospital at the weekend which provoked — or gave the prisoners the excuse — for the demonstration.

The staff will be disappointed if the man is not firmly dealt

with but a too severe sentence could provoke more reaction by the inmates.

Officers expect the troubles to die down for a few days. The Home Office threat of moves could cause some of the "barons" to lie low. It would take them a long time to re-establish themselves in another jail. And there is always the fear of segregation.

Demonstrations by prisoners continued at several of Britain's jails today.

At Peterhead, the 170 prisoners who began a roof-top protest yesterday were still perched on the prison hospital roof this morning after 22 hours without food.

Trouble spreads

Trouble in the jails spread today as more and more prisoners joined rooftop protests.

By lunchtime, at least seven prisons were affected by demonstrations, while at an eighth — Hull's top security jail — 53 prisoners were staging a work strike.

A look around showed:
Chelmsford: Seven men sitting it out for the second day.
Parkhurst: 21 rebels on the roof.
Camp Hill, Isle of Wight: Three prisoners up aloft.
Walton, Liverpool: Two men on roof, with nearly 50 sitting down in exercise yards.
Peterhead, Aberdeen: 120 men on the second day of rooftop demonstration.
Stafford: Five protesters climbed onto a roof today and threatened to stay out for a week.
Cardiff: Another five unknown joined the rooftop rebels today.

Farm workers carry Prince's coffin

PRINCE William of Gloucester died in an air crash on Monday, was taken home, to the village of Barnwell in Northamptonshire today.

Only a few silent people assembled in the 13th century parish church as the heavy oak coffin was carried in by six workers from the royal estate at Barnwell Manor.

But villagers were expected to see the coffin before it is laid to rest.

The coffin will remain in the church until tomorrow afternoon when it will be taken to Windsor for private burial on Saturday.

See (about voting rules) Page 12).

Thief's goal was Filbert Street till

A THIEF was on the ball last night when he visited the Leicester City football ground for the City v Liverpool match.

As he paid his entrance fee into the double-decker stand he grabbed £85 from the cash desk at the turnstile and made off into a nearby crowd of fans.

A steward saw the culprit but was unable to tackle him as the thief slipped away by running through the stand, and out of the ground.

The thief is described — being 5ft. 7 inches tall, aged about 40 and wearing a brown sports jacket.

Mr. John Smith, secretary of the football club said although this sort of theft was not a common occurrence at the club it did happen last year when Leicester met Liverpool at home.

ON OTHER PAGES

● Planner's pledge to Groby
— Page 12

● Decision on future of Lutterworth—Page 27

TV and Radio Page 2

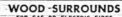

The *Leicester Mercury* front page noting the response of local civic leaders to the prospect of Ugandan Asians heading for Leicester. (*Leicester Mercury*)

Belgrave Road's 'Golden Mile', the heart of the Asian community in Leicester. The decorations mark the Hindu festival of Diwali (light). In the 1970s the British United Shoe Machinery Company was one of the largest employers of Asian labour. Today the site has been redeveloped as a commercial centre for Asian businesses. This photograph was taken from the top of the Belgrave Road flyover. (*Leicester Mercury*)

A Leicester Indian Worker's Association leaflet opposing immigration laws, 1980. A Nationality Bill (1980), which became the Nationality Act (1981), was criticized for reinforcing racial discrimination by excluding British overseas citizens (mostly Asian) from the right of abode in the UK. (*Val Marett*)

Ajmer Singh Matharu just before his retirement, Highfields, 1989. He was a deputy superintendent of police from 1956 to 1969 in Uganda and became a British officer in 1970. He was the first Asian police officer in Leicester. (*Ajmer Singh Matharu*)

2

Education

Children at Uplands Junior School, 1967. In 2000 the school was nominated by the City Council for beacon status as a mark of its contribution to education. Uplands School is at the heart of the Highfields area, the first part of Leicester to be populated by the Asian community. Many of the pictures in this chapter focus on it and the contribution it has made to the community. (*Uplands School*)

The arrival of Ugandan refugees in the 1970s resulted in dramatic changes in the pupils attending many inner-city schools. The school building programme was held back because Leicester City Council, unlike the County Council, could not formally agree on which form of comprehensive school system it wished to adopt. In spite of the subsequent scattering of the Asian community, many inner-city schools continued to have a high proportion of immigrants in their classes. A significant number of Asian students entered higher education and became important role models for the community. The importance of the Asian community has also been recognized by the appointment of several leading figures to senior positions within the education system.

Children at Uplands School, 1960s. This class of children from different ethnic backgrounds was typical of this area of the city. (*Uplands School*)

Children from Uplands School with their teacher, 1960s. (*Uplands School*)

A group of children dressed for a play outside Uplands School, 1960s. The photograph shows the typical terraced properties that predominate in this part of the city. (*Uplands School*)

Children from Uplands School at a summer camp organized by teachers, 1960s. (*Uplands School*)

Author Gurharpal Singh (left), formerly Professor of Indian Politics at the University of Hull and now Professor of Inter-Faith Relations at the University of Birmingham, enjoying a school dinner with his brother Gurpritpal in the 1960s. Gurpritpal is now a leading consultant with Microsoft. (*Gurharpal Singh*)

Baroness Usha Prashar, Chancellor of De Montfort University, opening the refurbished Clephan Building, 2000. Baroness Prashar came to the United Kingdom from Kenya in 1964 to study. She is chairman of the Parole Board of England and Wales, deputy chairman of the National Literacy Council and a non-executive director of Channel 4. Left to right: Professor Judy Simons, High Sheriff of Leicestershire Anthony Wessel, Lord Mayor of Leicester Councillor Barbara Chambers, Vice-Chancellor Professor Philip Tasker, Baroness Prashar, Lady Mayoress Heather Chambers and Caroline Wessel. (*De Montfort University*)

Children from Uplands School participating in a Radio Us one-off broadcast, 1970s. (*Uplands School*)

Staff at Uplands School, early 1970s. Clifton Robinson (front row, third from left) was the first immigrant primary school headmaster in the district. (*Uplands School*)

A music teacher with one of his pupils, both of them in Punjabi Bhangra costume, 1970s. The teacher is playing a dhol drum. (*Uplands School*)

Two newly arrived refugee pupils from Uganda with their Leicester-born classmates at Latimer High School in Belper Street, 6 February 1973. (*Leicester Mercury*)

Mellor Primary School, 1969. This picture illustrates the multi-cultural composition of the class. (*Mellor Primary School*)

Children from Leicester High School reading to younger pupils books which they have written themselves, 1997. (*Leicester High School*)

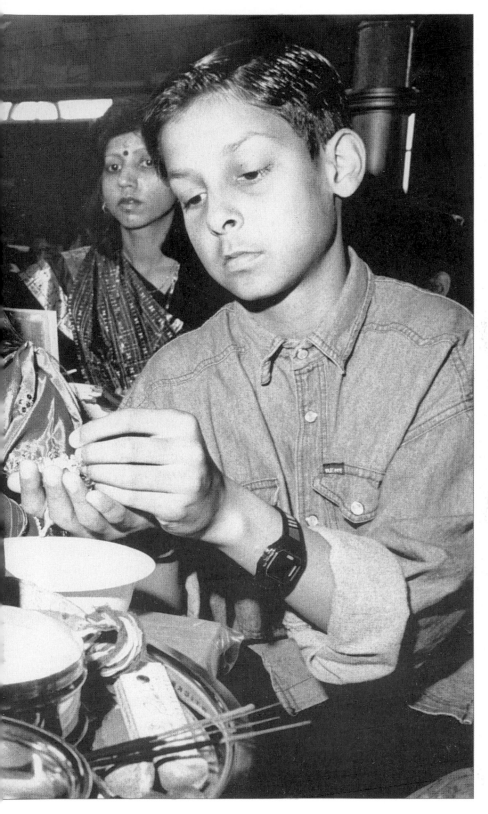

Children at a
religious story-telling
event focused on the
importance of truth
in Hinduism held at
the Shree Sanatan
Mandir, 1993.
(*Leicester Mercury*)

Police involvement with schoolchildren, like these at Uplands in the early 1970s, was seen as an important way of improving community relationships. (*Uplands School*)

Bob Parsons, who played the Demon Headmaster on BBC television, meeting children from Uplands Junior School, November 1997. (*Uplands School*)

Freda Hussain, front row second from right, head of the Moat Community College, with pupils and staff. She was the first Asian head of a secondary school in Leicester. (*Freda Hussain*)

Teacher Asaf Hussain, fourth from right, visiting a mosque with students. Asaf (husband of Freda who is pictured above) is an independent tutor and is active among voluntary groups in the city. (*Freda Hussain*)

De Montford University, Leicester has a significant Asian student population, many of whom come from colleges and schools within the city. This picture shows a business studies lecture in progress. (*De Montfort University*)

Muslim prayer facilities at the Leicester campus of De Montfort University. Religious support at the university reflects the varying faiths of a community of more than 20,000 students. (*De Montfort University*)

3

Sport & Leisure

Ajmer Singh Matharu with his Belgrave hockey team training at Rushey Mead, mid-1970s. The highly successful team won numerous championships. (*Ajmer Singh Matharu*)

Leisure activities constitute an important part of all cultures. In Leicester's Asian community leisure time is filled with diverse activities ranging from visits to tourist attractions to participation in traditional sports.

Many sections of the Asian community have been successful in establishing clubs and organizations to promote sport. Hockey, cricket, football and kabbadi (Punjabi wrestling) are among the most popular.

A family in Blackpool, 20 October 1956. Blackpool was an attractive holiday venue for all nationalities at this time. Formal dress tended to predominate during this period. (*Manjit Singh Rano*)

Marcus Solanki, his mother and father on a day trip to Alton Towers, 1968. Marcus is now a care officer in an old people's home. (*Marcus Solanki*)

An Asian family standing next to their newly acquired van during a day trip, 1965. (*Manjit Singh Rano*)

Mrs Solanki and her son in their sitting room, 1968. In the background is their black and white television, a form of entertainment then growing in popularity. (*Marcus Solanki*)

The Darpan Arts Group about to perform a stick dance at the Gujarat Hindu Association's annual Ras Garba festival held at De Montfort Hall, 1978. (*Leicester Mercury*)

Nilima Devi, one of the leading exponents of kathak dance. Kathak is the classic dance style from northern India. Nilima runs a dance school in the city. (*Nilima Devi*)

Girls performing the traditional Indian Ras Garba folk dances, 1991. (*Leicester Mercury*)

Children from Uplands Junior School performing at the Royal Albert Hall, November 1998. In the words of the *Times Educational Supplement*, 13 November 1998: 'Perhaps the most abiding memory of the evening was the spectacle of the Leicestershire massed choir with more than 500 singers . . . this was entertainment on a grand scale. Even Hollywood could not have done it better.' (*Uplands Junior School*)

The Indian National Hockey Team visiting Leicester after the 1968 Olympics. The team played an exhibition match against the Indian Sports Association at Saffron Lane stadium. (*Gurharpal Singh*)

A fun run and race organized by the Belgrave-based Khalsa Club, 1987. More than 500 runners took part in the event which began in Victoria Park. (*Leicester Mercury*)

A city kabaddi team, 1992. Kabaddi is a wrestling game played by two teams. It developed in northern India and is extremely popular among Punjabis in Leicester. (*Leicester Mercury*)

A kabaddi team from Kenya who played in a tournament organized by the Indian Sports Association, 1976. (*Gurharpal Singh*)

A hockey team coached by Ajmer Singh Matharu, mid-1970s. (*Ajmer Singh Matharu*)

Sport has been used as a means to tackle racism. Left to right: Dion Dublin, Piara Singh Claire (Leicester city councillor), Emile Heskey. (*Sital Gill*)

A 24-hour sponsored pool event raised nearly £2,000 for the Indian earthquake disaster appeal in 1993. (*Leicester Mercury*)

Members of Leicester Overseas Cricket Club who organized an Indian Independence Day dance in 1987. They are pictured with the Lord Mayor of Leicester Janet Setchfield and Keith Vaz MP. The club was established in the 1970s. (*Leicester Mercury*)

Sir John Cadman, Director of the England Hockey Association, talking to the team coached by Ajmer Singh Matharu at the Sikh Sports festival held on the eve of Baisakhi, 1976. (*Ajmer Singh Matharu*)

The festival of Baisakhi or Vaisakhi marks the dawn of a new year in northern India and for Sikhs it is a formal celebration of their brotherhood and community. Among the events held in Leicester to mark the festival is the annual sports contest. Teams from across the country took part in the two-day Vaisakhi sports festival at Victoria Park, London Road, in May 1986. (*Leicester Mercury*)

Strongman Manjit Singh shows members of The Bodybuilding Gym based at the Guru Teg Bahadur Gurdwara community centre on East Park Road how to use the pull-up bar, 1993. (*Leicester Mercury*)

4

Places of Worship

Gathering for prayers at a mosque in Highfields, 1990s. (*Leicester Council of Faiths*)

In the mid-nineteenth century Leicester had many churches attended by worshippers of various denominations. As people moved away from the central business district and church attendance declined, many fell into disrepair and some were demolished or adapted for secular purposes. The increase in the size of the Asian population has led to a revival in the number of places of worship in the city.

The Asian community's first places of worship in Leicester were established in residential areas. This is the Hindu temple in Cromford Street in the early 1970s. (*Leicester Mercury*)

A procession to mark the opening of the Hindu temple in Cromford Street, 1969. (*Leicester Mercury*)

In the 1980s the former Congregational church on Oxford Street became a centre for Jainism, an ancient religion that teaches love for all living creatures. The building contains fifty-two hand-carved pillars, a hand-carved ceiling and stained-glass windows. Chandulal Trivedi of Ahmedabad in Gujarat was the mason charged with carving the pillars from Rajastan stone. (*Leicester Mercury*)

Detail from a hand-carved limestone pillar inside the Jain Centre. (*Jain Centre*)

A stained-glass window from the Jain Centre. It shows Mahavir seeking permission of his brother Nandivardhan to renounce the world so that he can find the path for happiness for all living beings. (*Jain Centre*)

A Jain procession making its way down Welford Road, 1985. (*Leicester Mercury*)

Inside the Jain temple, 1985. (*Leicester Mercury*)

Jains celebrating the anniversary of the opening of their temple, July 1991. (*Leicester Mercury*)

The first stage of the domed roof of the Central Mosque being installed in October 1989. (*Leicester Mercury*)

An aerial view of the Highfields area showing the Central Mosque in the foreground. (*Vasant Kalyani*)

Muslims offering prayers to mark Eid-al-Adha, one of the most important festivals in the Islamic calendar, 1992. The festival comes at the end of the Hajj pilgrimage. (*Leicester Mercury*)

The Central Mosque in Conduit Street is the largest in Leicester and the main focus for Friday prayers for the Muslim community in the city. (*Leicester Council of Faiths*)

The Al-Bukhari Mosque, Loughborough Road, opened in 1985 and was the second purpose-built mosque in Leicester. (*Leicester Mercury*)

A corner of Victoria Park was used in 1989 by Muslims who gathered to pray and celebrate Eid-al-Adha, the festival of sacrifice. It is regarded as the most important event in the Islamic calendar and marks the end of the pilgrimage to Mecca. The festival highlights obedience to God in the same way as the account in the scriptures of Ibrahim offering to sacrifice his own son to Allah. (*Leicester Mercury*)

A Shia Muslim procession along Belgrave Road in 1994, during Muharram to commemorate the martyrdom of the Prophet Mohammed's grandson Husain. (*Leicester Mercury*)

The elegant newly built Masjid Umar on Evington Road, 2001. (*Faiyazuddin Ahmad*)

The exterior of the Sri Sanatan Prarthna Mandir (Hindu temple) at the corner of Westcotes Drive and Narborough Road. (*Vasant Kalyani*)

Inside the Shree Swaminarayan Temple, Loughborough Road, 2001. (*Vasant Kalyani*)

Deities at the Shree Swaminarayan
Temple in Loughborough Road,
1992. (*Vasant Kalyani*)

A white marble carving imported
from India being cleaned at the
Shree Sanatan Mandir and
Community Centre. The increase in
the Indian population of Leicester
led to the establishment in the
1970s of the city's first Hindu
temple. In the following decade it
became a centre of worship
recognized throughout the United
Kingdom. (*Vasant Kalyani*)

A typical weekend congregation at the Shree Sanatan Mandir Hindu temple, 1984. (*Leicester Mercury*)

A Sikh granthi reading from the holy scripture of Guru Granth Sahib at Sri Guru Ravidas Gurdwara, Harrison Road, 1998. (*Ajmer Singh Matharu*)

The flag changing ceremony in 1987 at the Guru Tegh Bahadur Sikh temple in East Park Road to mark baisakhi, the most important event in the Sikh calendar. More than 12,000 Leicester Sikhs participated in the anniversary. (*Leicester Mercury*)

Leading members of the Sikh community helping to raise the new flag at the Guru Tegh Bahadur temple on East Park Road in 1990. Sikhs and Hindus celebrate the New Year with a month-long festival called Vaisakhi. For the Sikhs the festival begins with a day of prayer followed by a 48-hour recital of Sikh holy scriptures. (*Leicester Mercury*)

Entrance to the Guru Teg Bahadar gurdwara on East Park Road, 1992. The words in Gurmukhi begin with *ek onkar*, signifying the oneness of God, and state the name and address of the gurdwara. (*Leicester Mercury*)

Sikhs from all the temples of Leicester joining together for a peaceful procession to mark Vaisakhi, 1993. (*Leicester Mercury*)

5

Festivals, Events & Celebrations

Belgrave Mela, 1990. In India a mela is a traditional social festival held at the end of the harvest. The Belgrave Mela is now a regular event which attracts people from all over the city. (*Leicester Mercury*)

Religious commemoration is the inspiration for virtually all the major festivals in Leicester. A common feature is the celebration of either the birth or death of a religion's founder or some other decisive event in the development of the faith in question. The knowledge that other followers throughout the world are also celebrating helps reinforce the feeling of belonging to the particular religion. Festivals are a key factor in creating community spirit and are part of a social drama in which everyone can take part, even if only as a spectator. Since the Second World War Leicester has become one of the major multicultural cities of Britain.

The Sikh religion started in the fifteenth century in the area of Pakistan and north-west India called the Punjab, which means land of five rivers. It was founded by Guru Nanak (1469–1539) and expanded under the leadership of Nanak's nine successors, each of whom was called Guru. In 1699 the last, Guru Gobind Singh, created the Khalsa – the concept of a saint and soldier whose duties related to prayers and singing hymns but also to taking part in sports in order to ensure his physical fitness for the defence of the less fortunate. In 1708 after the death of Guru Gobind Singh the focus of authority was transferred from the gurus to the sacred scripture, the Guru Granth Sahib, which is the holy book of Sikhism. This picture shows the Panj Pyares, or Five Beloved Ones, leading a procession of 4,000 Sikhs during Vaisakhi celebrations in 1993. (*Leicester Mercury*)

The Panj Pyares leading a procession in 1990. (*Leicester Mercury*)

A Sikh temple is called a gurdwara ('the Guru's door'). The sacred scripture is located here and this is the place where Sikhs gather. (*Leicester Mercury*)

A guru is a spiritual teacher or guide who awakens a disciple to the realization of his own divine nature. In Sikh religion the term is applied to the ten teachers from Guru Nanak to Guru Gobind Singh. (*Leicester Mercury*)

Celebrations in Belgrave Road to mark Diwali, the festival of lights, 1985. For Hindus Diwali commemorates the return of Rama from exile and his reunion with Sita, as explained in the Mahabharata. For Sikhs it marks the release from prison of the sixth Guru and his return to the golden city of Amritsar. (*Leicester Mercury*)

Diwali celebrations in Belgrave Road, 1995. (*Leicester Mercury*)

A City Council worker installing Diwali decorations. Belgrave Road had become the commercial heart of the Asian community by the 1990s. It is now known as the Golden Mile. (*Leicester Mercury*)

The burning of the effigy of Ravana, the demon king, marks Dussehra, literally the tenth day following the ninth night of Navratri. The Hindu ceremony takes place at the Cossington Street Recreation Ground each year, and this one was photographed in 1998. In Britain the festival falls in the period September/October. (*Vasant Kalyani*)

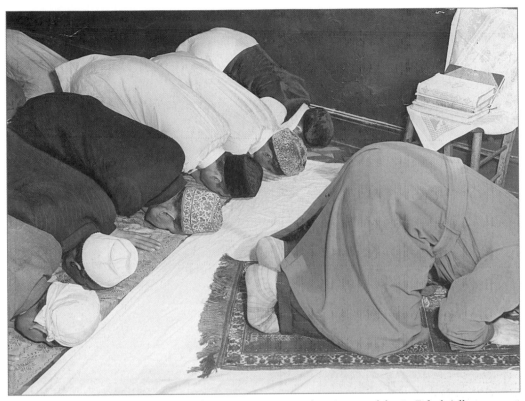

In 1954 seventeen Muslims gathered in a restaurant in the city to celebrate Eid-al-Adha, a great festival, for the first time in Leicester. Eid-al-Adha is held to commemorate the prophed Ibrahim's readiness to sacrifice his son Ismail in obedience to Allah. (*Leicester Mercury*)

Muslim women and children gathering to celebrate the birthday of the prophet Mohammed, 1989. (*Leicester Mercury*)

During the month of Muharram, Shiite Muslims identify themselves with the suffering of Husain, the grandson of Mohammed, and vilify his persecutors. They commemorate the death of Husain in the Battle of Karbala. Here followers in Leicester take part in a procession from the Loughborough Road mosque to the Belgrave flyover and back, 1997. (*Vasant Kalyani*)

A service to commemorate the anniversary of the birthday of Lord Shri Krishna in the Shree Sanatan Mandir Temple, Weymouth Street, 1979. The festivities continued after the service with traditional folk dancing and singing by young members of the temple. (*Leicester Mercury*)

A priest from the Shree Sanatan Mandir at the New Year's Day Jalaram bhagans held at the Shree Ram Mandir, Belgrave, in 1995. This event, which is held on the first Sunday of the month, happened to coincide with the first day of the New Year. (*Leicester Mercury*)

A procession of Leicester's Hindus. The chariot contains an image of Lord Krishna and the event, held on Melton Road in 1982, marked the Ratha-Yatra festival. (*Leicester Mercury*)

Swaminarayan Mission celebrating Annakut, meaning 'mountain of food', at the Soar Valley Sports Hall in 1991. This picture shows only a small section of this 'harvest festival' display. (*Leicester Mercury*)

Lighting the bonfire to mark the beginning of the Hindu festival of Holi, the advent of spring, at the Shree Shakti Mandir Temple in Moira Street, 1982. (*Leicester Mercury*)

Actors portraying
Hindu characters
including King
Dashratu and the
queens Kaushaliya,
Sumitra and Kaikai,
1993. (*Leicester
Mercury*)

Shree Hindu temple and community centre members celebrating Holi by lighting bonfires. The event is accompanied by prayers and marks the victory of Prahlad, a devotee of Lord Vishnu, who, according to Hindu belief, survived fires, floods and poison in his devotion to God. (*Leicester Mercury*)

Members of the Shree Bardai Brahma Samaj Hindu community dancing around a shrine during the festival of Navratri, 1985. Navratri (meaning nine nights) has a feminine theme. (*Leicester Mercury*)

Members of the Shree Sanatan Mandir parading the shrine that is the focal point for the Navratri festival, October 1985. (*Leicester Mercury*)

Ratha-Yatra chariot journey, 2000. Devotees push huge wagons (rathas) supporting images of Krishna. He is known by the name 'jagannatu', meaning Lord of the Universe and the origin of the English word juggernaut. The festival is organized by the International Society for Krishna Consciousness. (*Leicester Council of Faiths*)

An event to mark International Women's Day organized by the City Council's Corporate Equalities team in the late 1990s. Asian women were leading figures in the movement to develop specific events marking women's contribution to business and the community in Leicester. Councillor Manjula Sood is holding the microphone and on the right is Angela Berryman, the city's first Faiths Project Officer. (*Leicester City Council*)

The author Sue Townsend launching the Leicester Literature Festival on 21 October 1998 with children from Uplands Junior School. (*Uplands School*)

The Lord and Lady Mayoress of Leicester, a representative of the High Commissioner of Pakistan and Keith Vaz MP with Jim Marshall MP at a celebration to mark Pakistan's independence day, 1989. (*Leicester Mercury*)

Members of the Leicestershire Pakistani Association marking the organization's silver jubilee and the thirty-eighth anniversary of Pakistan's independence at a meeting at Moat Community College in 1985. (*Leicester Mercury*)

Protesters opposed to novelist Salman Rushdie's novel *Satanic Verses* marching from Spinney Hill Park, 1989. Evington Road cinema, one of the best known in Leicester, is on the left. It has since been converted into flats for elderly Asians by ASRA (see p. 121). (*Leicester Mercury*)

Gujarat Hindu Association marking Indian Independence Day with a flag hoisting ceremony at Belgrave Neighbourhood Centre, 1993. (*Leicester Mercury*)

Members of Leicester Indian Workers Association before an anti-racism march through London in 1993. They marched past the headquarters of the British National Party. (*Sital Gill*)

Members of the Indian Workers Association march past the Houses of Parliament, *c.* 1978. (*Sital Gill*)

6

The Family

Indian weddings are vibrant and colourful events famed for their feasts
and spectacular processions. Here Ravi Sood and his nephew Manish
take part in a traditional wedding procession in 1992. The bride and
bridegroom are riding a white horse.

The family is central to the Asian way of life. Most social
activity revolves around it and the extended family is recognized as a great source of strength at home and in business.

A Hindu (left) and a Muslim (below) wedding invitation. In a Hindu wedding ceremony rice is always thrown as a blessing, and represents the bride's life. (*Christians Aware, 1997*)

A Sikh wedding ceremony. A relative is giving her blessing before the recital of the wedding rites. (*Christians Aware, 1997*)

The newly wed couple at *ardas* (prayer) after the completion of the wedding ceremony. (*Christians Aware, 1997*)

An Asian family at a Church of England wedding. The Solankis are one of a small number of Christian Asian families in Leicester. (*Marcus Solanki*)

About 1,500 guests attended the wedding of fashion designer Kawsari Begum Faki Mahmood and Iqbal Mohammed Shaffi Khan in Leicester in 1985. The bride's father, Faki Mahmood, was a Muslim community leader. (*Leicester Mercury*)

The central event of a Hindu wedding ceremony takes place around the sacred fire. The groom's mother ties a knot between the two scarves worn by the bride and groom, signifying the joining of the couple and the two families. (*Leicester Council of Faiths*)

The Basra family, 1966. The mother is third from the left and with her are her son and two daughters-in-law. The ornate bangles worn by the daughter-in-law second from the left are worn for the first five weeks of marriage. (*Baljinder Kaur*)

The Basra family outside their home in East Park Road, 1973. (*Baljinder Kaur*)

7

Work & Business

Mira Travedi, Radio Leicester presenter, *c.* 1976. In 1967 Radio
Leicester became the first BBC local radio station to hit the airwaves.
(*Radio Leicester*)

Historically Leicester's industry was based on hosiery,
knitwear and footwear manufacture but more recently it has
been focused on light engineering, printing and food
processing. However, even at a time of full employment
obtaining work was considerably more difficult for ethnic
minorities than for the indigenous population. The number
of second generation Asians who have secured white collar
employment has continued to increase although they still
remain under-represented in many areas, such as education,
the police and the civil service. Members of the Asian
community have also become entrepreneurs, running a
wide variety of businesses from corner shops and grocers to
supermarkets, jewellers, pharmacies and clothing stores.
Asian businesses also have a significant role in the
manufacturing sector, particularly in textiles. The majority
of Asian businesses are still run by family members.

Ajmer Singh Matharu in 1970 having completed the twelve-week initial training course for the police force at Ryton upon Dunsmore near Coventry. He is wearing the Queen's Medal, which was awarded to Ugandan officers who had completed more than twelve years' service with good conduct and had been forced to retire prematurely by Idi Amin. (*Ajmer Singh Matharu*)

Ajmer Singh Matharu talking with fellow officers after joining the Leicestershire and Rutland Constabulary. Asian men and women are still under-represented in the police force; both recruitment and retention are ongoing problems. (*Ajmer Singh Matharu*)

Sister Nirmala Solanki of Hillcrest Hospital, Leicester who was nominated as 'My Favourite Nurse' in a competition held in 1976. (*Marcus Solanki*)

Sanjay K. Chauhan working in his shoe shop, 1985. Family-run and hand-craft businesses account for a large proportion of Asian firms in Britain. (*Sanjay K. Chauhan*)

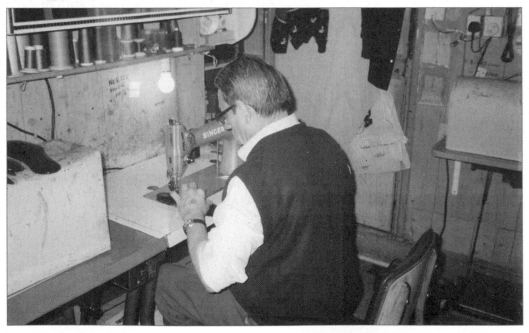

Kanji H. Chauhan, father of Sanjay, sewing ornate slippers in the back of the shop. Craft methods of production are still a feature of many Asian footwear shops. (*Sanjay K. Chauhan*)

Kartar Singh Sandhu, presenter and adviser to the producer of 'The 6.05 Show' on BBC Radio Leicester, *c.* 1977. (*Radio Leicester*)

Mira Travedi and Don Kotak, the original presenters of the 'Six Three O Show' on BBC Radio Leicester. (*Radio Leicester*)

Mark Tully, one-time BBC India correspondent, author, commentator and film-maker, with Mike Allbut and colleagues, Radio Leicester. (*Radio Leicester*)

Bhupinder Atwall, Radio Leicester presenter. (*Radio Leicester*)

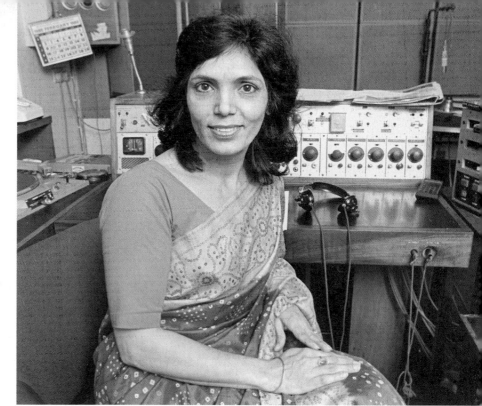

BBC Asian Service staff, 1997. Seated: Sujahu Bard, Rabin Raza, Vijay Sharma and Nerrha Kara. Second row: Amir Khan, Niraj Samani, two production assistants, Mehesh Netwuni and Sajjad Karim. Back row: Hesam Muquaddam, Mike Allbut, Deepak Patel and Kamlish Purhit. (*BBC Radio Leicester*)

Vijay Sharma, Editor of the BBC Asian Network which broadcasts in the Midlands, and network staff, 1998. Its programmes are also available across the UK on digital satellite services and on the Internet. (*BBC Asian Network*)

A BBC Asian Network roadshow, 1997. (*BBC Asian Network*)

Hartington Road traders. In 1989 teenagers from the Hartington Road area turned the Hindu festival of Jagran into a massive charity bid by persuading traders to keep their businesses open throughout the night. Jagran marks the awakening of the Gujarah Hindu god. (*Leicester Mercury*)

Hartington Road. The Traders' Association banner advertises an all-night shopping spree to raise money for a number of local charities, July 1989. (*Leicester Mercury*)

Keith Vaz MP (third from left), Manjeet Tara (fourth from left), homeworkers and campaigners outside 10 Downing Street, October 1989. A petition was presented to Prime Minister Margaret Thatcher drawing attention to the fact that homeworkers in Britain earned £1 per hour or less. Manjeet Tara is a prominent campaigner on homeworking issues at local, national and international level. Her intervention has led to important national and European government changes affecting homeworkers. (*Manjeet Tara*)

After ten years of campaigning Manjeet Tara successfully negotiated the inclusion of homeworkers in the national minimum wage legislation. She is pictured here with Peter Gratidge from the Inland Revenue at a Department of Trade and Industry event in November 1999 to advise ethnic minorities about the minimum wage. (*Manjeet Tara*)

An Indian craftsman working on an ornamental display for one of the temples in the city. Many of the temples in Leicester often invite skilled craftsmen from India and elsewhere to design and complete displays. The Jain temple in Oxford Street was complete by craftsmen specialized in the Jain tradition of design and architecture. (*Leicester Mercury*)

Sue Waddington MEP and European staff meeting Asian business people. (*Paul Winstone*)

Staff at Chatham Printers, Chatham Street. The picture shows Mrs Poonam Naker whose husband Kirit founded the business. (*Vasant Kalyani*)

8

People & Places

In 1981 Kartar Singh Sandhu was made an MBE for services to community relations in Leicester. Mr Sandhu was a teacher at St Paul's RC School, Evington, an executive member of Leicester Council for Race Relations and secretary of the Sikh Education Council in Leicestershire. He is pictured outside Buckingham Palace with his wife and children, Ruby and Ranu. (*Kartar Singh Sandhu*)

The Asian community is well established in Leicester. It has more than 1,500 firms run by some of the leading businessmen and women in the city, and can boast two former Lord Mayors, numerous councillors and an MP. This section includes some of those individuals.

The first Asian Lord Mayor of Leicester, Gordon Parmar, enjoying fish and chips. He was Lord Mayor from 1987 to 1989. (*Leicester Mercury*)

Lord Mayor and Lady Mayoress Parmar with members of their family, 1987. (*Parmar family*)

Former Indian High Commissioner Kuldip Nayer with Leicester West MP Greville Janner on a visit to the Newfoundpool Neighbourhood Centre, 1992. (*Sital Gill*)

'Maz' Mashru, a well-known Leicester photographer, with a selection of his awards for his work. (*Leicester Mercury*)

Kartar Singh Sandhu, chairman of the pensioners' rights campaign, at a rally in London, 1998. (*Leicester Mercury*)

Gurdial Singh and Rughbir Singh performing at the bhangra club in Regents Road, 1965. The club was one of the first to be established in Leicester. Gurdial Singh was one of the founder members of the Indian Sports Association and a manager at Walker's Crisps, which recruited many newly arrived migrants.(*Gurharpal Singh*)

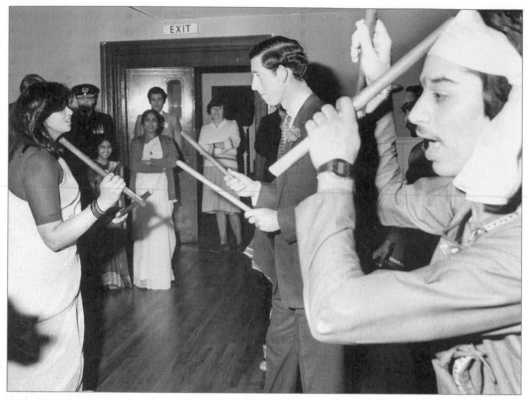

Prince Charles on a visit to the city, trying his hand at stick dancing, 1981. (*Leicester Mercury*)

Prince Charles talking to volunteers at the Belgrave Neighbourhood Centre. (*Leicester Mercury*).

Lalit Mansingh, the Indian High Commissioner, talking to a gathering, 1999. The other people on the platform are, left to right: Councillor Peter Swift (Lord Mayor), Patricia Hewitt MP and Councillor Peter Soulsby. (*Leicester City Council*)

Manjit Singh, ironman of Leicester, breaking the world record for baked bean eating, 1999. (*Leicester Mercury*)

Lata Mangeshkar at the Asian Song Contest, Haymarket Theatre, 1980. The competition was organized annually by Radio Leicester and here Lata Mangeshkar is announcing the awards. Lata is the leading Indian playback singer in Bollywood. (*BBC Radio Leicester*)

Councillor Paul Sood, Dr Debu Choudhary and a colleague, 1983. Paul Sood was responsible for introducing Indian music and dancing into the curriculum of Leicester's schools. (*Mrs Sood*)

Dr L.M. Singhvi, Indian High Commissioner, planting a tree to commemorate his visit to Leicester in 1993. As High Commissioner Dr Singhvi was a frequent visitor to Leicester. Upon his return to India he was nominated by the Bharatiya Janata Party (BJP) to the upper house of parliament. (*Leicester Mercury*)

Keith Vaz MP meeting Simi Grewal, a leading Indian film actress, at a film festival in Leicester, *c.* 1996. (*Leicester Mercury*)

L.K. Advoni, currently India's Minister for Home Affairs, speaking at a function organized by the Bharatiya Janata Party's (BJP) Leicester chapter in 1991. The BJP, which leads the coalition government in New Delhi and represents the state government in Gujarat, has a significant following among Leicester's Gujurati population. Several chief ministers of Gujurat have visited Leicester. (*Leicester Mercury*)

Faiyazuddin Ahmad (left), President of Leicester Council of Faiths and a prominent Muslim community leader, in his study with a guest. (*Faiyazuddin Ahmed*)

Councillor Bupendra Dave with Keith Vaz MP (back, third from right) and constituents introducing details of patients' rights at the Belgrave Neighbourhood Centre. (*Marcus Solanki*)

Marcus Solanki (seated, right), manager of Ashram, with a group of elderly people. In Gujerati *ashram* means 'restful place'. It was established in 1994 to provide a caring and homely environment for elderly Asian people who are too frail to live alone or need more care than their families can provide. (*Marcus Solanki*)

The exterior of Ashram. (*Marcus Solanki*)

The exterior of homes provided by the Asian Residential Housing Association (ASRA), part of the Midlands Housing Association, off Loughborough Road. The association was established in 1983 to provide accommodation for Asian people. (*Vasant Kalyani*)

Two elderly residents being served by staff in ASRA accommodation. (*Vasant Kalyani*)

Evington cinema, now converted into flats for elderly Asian people. (*Vasant Kalyani*)

Mobile meals service provided by ASRA. (*ASRA*)

Keith Vaz MP addressing a meeting to mark Health Day on Diabetes and Patient Rights organized by the Leicester Asian Elderly Health Forum, 1992. (*Leicester Mercury*)

Leading members of the city's Islamic community and guests visiting the newly opened Central Mosque to mark Ramadan in 1993. Left to right: Councillor Malik Salim, Councillor Peter Soulsby, Councillor Hanif Asmal, Haji Noormohamed Sheikh, Councillor Mustafa Kamal, Councillor Bupendra Dave, David Yates, Councillor Ramnik Kavia and Councillor Mir Juma. (*Leicester Mercury*)

Charnwood Primary School children on a guided tour of an exhibition at Highfields Community Centre illustrating the role of the Islamic mosque, how and when a Muslim prays, the pillars of faith and the Islamic approach to economics, politics and worship. This photograph was taken in 1995. (*Leicester Mercury*)

Keith Vaz MP meeting Prince Charles at a Leicester City Council function on training and employment. (*Paul Winstone/LCC*)

Opposite: In 1990 the Hindu Temple and Community Centre was attended by 350 people, including leaders of several Hindu communities and councillors, to celebrate the wedding of Lord Krishna to Tulsi. This bride-giving ceremony is celebrated on the eleventh day after Diwali. (*Leicester Mercury*)

Kishar Rajani (left) and his brother Mohalal of Dil Khush Sweet Mart with sweets they produced for Diwali, 1991. (*Leicester Mercury*)

Reverend Professor Richard Bonney, Department of History, University of Leicester, meeting members of the All Gaytatri Parwar (AGP), 1999. The AGP is based in Hardwar, India and is dedicated to the intercommunion of science and spirituality. (*Richard Bonney*)

The Maher community association receiving the Ras Cup from B.S. Attwal, 1993. Ramanbhai
Barber is on the right. The group beat seventeen others in the Ras Garba dance competition.
(*Leicester Mercury*)

Education Secretary Sir Keith Joseph and Shree Pramukh Swami Maharaj (right), spiritual leader of
Swaminarayan Hindus worldwide, 1985. (*Leicester Mercury*)

List of Contributors

The authors would like to thank the *Leicester Mercury*, Leicester City Council, De Montfort University and the following individuals for their support:

S. Faiyazuddin Ahmad, M. Sarfraz Ahmad, Sharad Bakhai, Richard Bonney, Barbara Butler, Sanjay K. Chauhan, Minou Cortazzi, Sital Gill, Angela Jagger, Nathubhai Jagjivan, Stuart Jennings, Graham Johnson, Vasant Kalyani, Baljinder Kaur, Ian Keil, Theresa Keil, John Lally, Val Marett, Paul Marett, R. Mashru, Ramesh Mehta, David Mitchell, Manzoor Moghal, T.V. Morjaria, Suleman Nagdi, Panikos Panayi, Mrs G. Parmar, Dulabhai Patel, Alan Race, Smita Shah, Ataullah Siddiqui, Kehar Singh, Manjit Singh, Ajmer Singh Matharu, Manjit Singh Rano, Kartar Singh Sandhu, Resham Singh Sandhu, Marcus Solanki, Manjula Sood, Manjeet Tara, Narendra Waghela, Paul Winstone, Steve White.

DR JOHN MARTIN is Principal Lecturer in Economic and Social History at De Montfort University. He is author of *The Development of Modern Agriculture* (Palgrave, 2000) and has contributed extensively to the *New Dictionary of National Biography* in his role of Research Associate.

PROFESSOR GURHARPAL SINGH has lived in Leicester since 1964, where he taught contemporary Asian studies at De Montfort University. In 1999 he move to the University of Hull to become Professor of Indian Politics. He is currently the Nadir Chair of Inter-religious Relations at the University of Birmingham.

REVEREND DAVID CLARK is pleased to have been able to support the authors in their efforts to produce this book. He is an Anglican priest, member of the Leicester Council of Faiths and Chair of the Society for Inter Cultural Understanding, Leicester (SICUL).